EAR

EARTHAM

Poems of Past and Present

WILLIAM FOOT

© William Foot, 2022

Published by John Aubin

A CIP catalogue record for this book is available from the British Library.

ISBN 978-1-7396959-2-7

Book layout and cover design by Clare Brayshaw

Prepared and printed by:

York Publishing Services Ltd
64 Hallfield Road
Layerthorpe
York YO31 7ZQ

Tel: 01904 431213

Website: www.yps-publishing.co.uk

INTRODUCTION

Many of the poems you will find here were written during the period of Covid lockdown. As travelling a distance was frowned upon by our commissars at that time, I restricted my country walking to those parts of the West Sussex Downs closest to me, in particular the area around the village of Eartham, tucked away in its hidden valley.

Eartham is the place where I would most like to live, if it were only possible – but regretfully unlikely ever to be the case. To the west, the village is overlooked by Long Down, a largely level plateau of open downland. Neolithic people mined flint here: you can still see the hollows of the shafts they dug. Lidar surveys have revealed how in the Iron Age period a chequerboard pattern of fields criss-crossed Long Down. A Roman road – Stane Street – on its way from Chichester to London cut across its northern end. After the Roman period, the plateau must have reverted to grassland, which was only ploughed up again during the Second World War.

West of Long Down can be seen the windmill on Halnaker Hill that Hilaire Belloc commemorated, recently restored. It stands within a Neolithic causewayed enclosure, perhaps the home of the flint miners on Long Down. To the east is wooded Nore Hill, the slopes of which still show the bumps and ridges of Iron Age and Roman period settlement.

The beauty of this landscape, with its historic and archaeological undertones, forms the basis of a number of my poems. I have long been fascinated by a sense of the past trembling upon the present, which I feel most strongly on Long Down.

Eartham, and its surroundings, provided inspiration for my verse, which is why I have borrowed the name as the title of my small book.

William Foot

August 2022

CONTENTS

Eartham	1
Past Light	4
On a Burial of the Late Iron Age Found in West Sussex	5
Varusschlacht	7
At Bignor Roman Villa	8
Reflections on the Excavation of a Roman Bath House	9
Stonehenge	12
The Mosaic	13
Roman Villa	19
Roman Road	21
Hat Hill	23
The Burial	25
Stane Street	27
Whiteways Plantation	29
The Coin	31
Herculaneum	33
The Stag	34
Earth, Rock, Light	35
We Weep for the Dinosaurs	36
Old Photograph	37
Beneath the Trees	38
Funeral	40
The Veteran	41
The Lady Chapel, Ely Cathedral	43

People Watching 44

More Bloody Sun 45

The Rain 47

The Storm 48

Within the Shadowed Downs 50

Wondering 51

Reflection – Trundle Hill 52

Long Down 53

Boyhood 1950s 54

Littleworth Common 56

The Passing 58

Remembrance 60

Eartham Hill 61

The Beach 62

Peace 64

Recollections from Boyhood 65

Fear 67

Walberton House 68

Clouds 70

The Escape 71

On the Hottest Day 74

The Last Rabbit 76

The World Has Ceased its Tune 77

This England Now 79

Virus Town, March 2020 81

To the Next Big War 83

Horatius 2022 85

What They Have Done 86

War   88

On Eartham Long Down   89

I Have Seen a Country   90

A Summer Morning in England Still   91

Binsted   92

In Furrey Time   94

Furrey Time Forever   97

In Memory of a Jack Russell   100

The Skylark   101

Visions   102

To Edward Thomas   103

Fallen Poet   105

The Lamb   106

Helplessness   107

The Fly   108

Report to the Doctor   109

Rhyme   110

On Receiving the Results of a Poetry Competition   111

I'm Done with Words   112

When the Queen Died   113

EARTHAM

When you come here, it is yesterday:
the Down rises above like a scolding frown;
paths run away to nowhere and beyond;
none return, so beware which one you take
to reach this spot, this place of earth –
the name should tell you all, so be prepared –
the church at least is firmly set, with spire and font,
and facing heads upon the chancel arch,
so too the vicarage across the one small street,
it has a garden, the borders laid with vines;
they grow grapes there still,
the vicar drinks them with his prayers.

Beyond, above the hills, skies are swept
by wide, sailing clouds that bless the fields
with rain at Easter, and oft times in between
to Christmas, when the frosts are fierce like tigers' teeth:
once they mined the Down for flint, those ancient men,
who slew the stags with bows, you see their hollows
pressing at the grassy slopes, from where they say
Old Meg herself emerges when the moon rides high,
on bats' wings to milk the silent stars
and plump her withered breasts.

Here is yesterday,
when all is returned to us
in past light fusing with the present day,
for time can come to us in stops and starts
like a drunken man who weaves his way,

and stumbles from the eager stream
that bubbles on towards infinity:
he has no business there, no knowledge of extinction,
and does not wish to make such journey yet,
thrust out towards finality,
but rather seek out places that he knows,
most familiar, hoping to find them as he left,
bathed with fondling sun to warm his bones.

In truth, ghosts are very obstinate;
they will trail back home,
regardless of time's long ticking motion;
we can see their faces white amongst the trees
where the old road treads by;
Roman feet can be heard there, it is said,
when the dulled business of the day is done,
and the old deeds return, to be played out once more
in laughter and romance,
and in fear too, if we are honest.
So let it be.

Today is yesterday:
the pond is full;
green weed trails the surface,
orange fish with pursed mouths glide beneath,
the coloured wings of butterflies dart from out the flowers;
the sun is hot: the vicar's wife
bats her ball at tennis, the roses smell red and sweet:

at The George, the drinkers stand beside the lane,
pint pots in hand, the language is of England,
this, here and now;
what they do in London concerns them not,
or the wider world, what empires come and go:

the sound of creaking wheels, the blacksmith's hammer,
the flash of scythe, the shepherd with his flock at dawn,
all is known, all understood,
these weary tasks of living, each man controls his fate,
each woman too, often bolder than the man,
once all that eager wooing has been done:
they seek no aid, provided they have strength,
and limbs and mind are sound;
if not, then who knows? Parson might if he were here;
he is away with the gentry right now,
carrying a gun and shooting through the copse;
that's not parson's work, it's said:
his curate bears the Cross this Easter:
he is a good young man, it seems,
clever, they say, he has filled his head
with learning Cambridge-way.
What does he here then?
God only knows.

Our day was then and always:
it would never change
or be abdicated to some other state,
when all that is valued is removed,
or turned inside out, so truths are lies
and falsehood good;
and so the roundabout turns on,
but who are they coming to the fair? –
we shall not know until they are here.

Do we wish to know?
All will become clear.

PAST LIGHT

The past is light:
each small refraction, a million years
of living and dying;
all the myriad moments of fear and sorrow;
wars refought, the endless motions of hating,
seared into our temples of stone,
from where they may rise again like ghosts,
if we choose to see:

the light of the past shall never fade,
it is always here.

ON A BURIAL OF THE LATE IRON AGE FOUND IN WEST SUSSEX

This pale orb of bone
could have spoken to us once
and told us who he was,
whether King Commius,
or some other man of blood,
riding these fields,
his crested helm so filled with light,
a golden lace, that twists and turns and intertwines,
that surely it is the very radiance of the sun,
torn from the sky, that passes by –
the reed birds are startled into rushing flight,
even the wild boar turns in sudden fright.

Yet there are no lips now to talk, no tongue to say
who this man was, whose bed of clay was found
close by a roundabout (built since) some miles from Bognor
   Town:
we swoop by in painted boxes
scarce bigger than the iron-bound coffer
in which he was laid, for that journey of eternity
we too must face.

King Commius – if you it is
whose bones lie here, preserved in glass,
beneath these glaring lights
where our beetle faces swoon and stare,

our brains heavy with interpretation,
you who rode out to war
when Caesar was in our Island,
who saw the land burning,
the dark lines forming, marching, turning,
the skies raining steel –

then, for all we have done to you,
disturbing your long rest,
I hope your spirit still flows free...
    somewhere in our Sussex hills,
    in sunlight, wind and rain.

VARUSSCHLACHT

(Kalkriese, AD9 – 2019)

Light and darkness
move in shadows
through taut-tipped grass
that spears at legs,
unguarded
where only rain falls on our heads,
no storm now of steel and lead
swept here in torrential pestilence.

Can you see this scene?
Can you sense it through the echo chambers
of your brain?
to hear lost sounds,
those of many men assailed,
severed and spitted in bloody waste,
dying,
once the strongest and most proud.

Can you glimpse their light again
that still must tremble within this earth and rock?

or else you must read it
in your fancy fiction,
how Marius saved the Eagle –

only here he was quite unable.

AT BIGNOR ROMAN VILLA

Quintus Horatius Flaccus
(or Horace, as we know him now)
would have found it most droll
that his country mouse still lively makes its quest
with whiskered nose and curious ear
over the paving of a Roman house
(at least the last, poor ruins of one)
two thousand years from blunting his pen
by writing of the self-same thing
that I have witnessed today –
    two tiny, frightened eyes,
    one for each millennium past,
    are fastened on an escape that never comes,
    or ever can;
    the poor mouse falls back, every time
    it leaps to climb,
    and I share its fear, wanting its escape,
    unable to help:

there is no way I can be involved;
I cannot reach down to the mosaic
that imprisons it:
a young man's head is outlined there,
one of the seasons, I think,
summer probably, for he has a red nose;
perhaps he stood too long in the sun
before the dark earth fell upon him,
    and mouse and man.

REFLECTIONS ON THE EXCAVATION OF A ROMAN BATH HOUSE

(in Priory Park, Chichester, 2021)

We are lucky this year;
the sun stands yellow on the grass,
and it has not rained for days:
like a tribe of badgers
we have burrowed at the earth
and laid it open in blocks and squares,
by sections and layered walls of soil,
that are all labelled now and pegged as if to hold them there,
so they will not escape into time again
and fly from our reckoning:

above them our leader stands
his brown builders' boots and hi-viz vest
making his dominance clear,
this Caesar of the hour,
a pole in his hand, striped in red –
of our blood perhaps, we who have toiled here –
which surely he must wish to cast at
the goggling heads who watch him,
lined up so eagerly by the fence:

three score of them have come from out the town,
some with children on their back,
with gleeful shouts riding to the show like centaurs,
the elderly amongst them, more suitably sombre,
for any contemplation of the past by them is serious;

already they sense the sonorous tread of bleak mortality,
soon to enter that same dark tunnel
as those who lived here these long ages past,
and left their ash for us to pare away.

The Romans are our favourites,
they are always popular,
we feel we know them very well;
all watching here have viewed a hundred films
of racing chariots and steel-casqued legions,
of flowing silks and jewelled hands,
clasping wine goblets, in opulence,
lounging by some rippling pool,
carved of white marble, while torches burn
on into the night: they are never put out,
unlike life's own brief, flickering light:

our Caesar with his javelin
knows how to pitch his own story
into this credence; he has the bath house
that we have dug out of the flinty clay
of which to tell his audience;
they are eager for his words;
there are steamy waters to blow across their vision
and bathing hunks of men, tanned and glistening,
white-fleshed ladies too perhaps on special days;
even the grimy slave lighting the furnace fire
in night's black void before the cock has crowed;

his tales are good, the listeners follow him with their eyes;
he explains the heated floor with its piles of brick,

the fragments of walls, some mere powder now,
and shows them where the boiler may have stood,
although there is no trace of it at all;
the wrecking gangs were here, you see,
when still the rule of Rome was strong;
likely, the bath house stone has made a yard of city wall
that runs beyond the cricket pitch,
or was built up later for the priory church nearby –
for a modest thousand pounds or two, paid to the town,
you can be married there today,
and think of those who have gone before you and done the
    same:
they tried criminals there once as well,
and sent them up the road to be hanged;

for life can be a foul and ugly thing:
a bath house may keep our bodies clean,
but not our souls, which only time's
deep remorselessness may cleanse,
when we come to the ending of all things
that can claim consciousness
or speak of it –

and what then?

STONEHENGE

Time has leached the light
from out these stones;
they stand under the moon
like a giant's dead fingers;
the wind picks at them and turns away,
defeated.

Yet light is all about me under the drifting stars,
which fill my eyes with brilliance,
as remote from this priestly circle
as the fires of Sirius, Capella, and Orion
that were shining out when these rocks
were still pressed deep beneath the ocean,
long before anything was born,
or suckled milk at its mother's breast,
or had ancestors to be worshipped
or raised up gods in whose idols we could bury our reason.

I shall come here at dawn,
treading the white coils of the serpent,
raising my arms and chanting my praises,
to see how the new sun fires the sky
and burns upon the stones,
to give them life.

Then, of all things, I might know
the beginning and the end,
finding (as Eliot has imagined),
they are exactly the same.

THE MOSAIC*

Some mocking muse of time
has brought forth from the dull, dun earth
this coloured wonder,
a banquet for our vision, a feast
laid for us upon a patterned carpet,
which four round-limbed men,
telamones – as we learn their name –
raise up by its corners:
they have waited these many centuries
to come into our light.

We gather here at the trench edge,
looking down,
our legs in cloth-rolled tubes,
some, bare and brown,
above which, the restless cylinders of our bodies
are crowned by nodding heads,
an indication surely of our absorption,
as we seek to follow what the good professor speaks,
who stands before us,
his feet stamped firmly in Caesar's Rome,
while we hover above, uneasily,
our crowded, drive-by world of telly and pop –
the hurling noise of which has smudged
the comprehension of our brains
like ill-brushed chalk –
distant from him by fifteen hundred years, or so.

---

* *discovered at Boxford, Berkshire*

His hands cast shadows upon the past:
he spreads them, pointing, over the cubed floor
with its swirling loops of *tesserae,*
its triangles and squares and curving lines,
showing how they make bold arms and heads,
a horse and lion, a rider in a flowing cloak,
an armed man with a shield, another with a bow,
an urn spilling fronds, a square-set throne,
all pictures painted out upon the ground,
which now we can see clearly,
if not yet understand.

The horseman is Bellerophon, our expert says,
on his winged mount, Pegasus;
can you see how he is stabbing his lance
at one of the fiery mouths of the Chimaera –
a foul enemy, a pestilence on the land?
this device was also taken into war
by those red devils falling from the air,
who grappled with the selfsame beast
within the lifetime of our fathers;
and certainly, as you suggest, sir
(one of us has ventured comment),
it could be seen as St. George who fights the dragon,
for this was the imagery of Christians too –
the light that pierces darkness,
the final triumph over death:

and here you can find the fatal contest
when Myrtilus caused King Oenomous' chariot
to crash – he removed a linchpin from its wheels –
though Pelops took the prize

of Hippodemia's beauty for himself;
see, she stands with her robe lowered,
her favours clear;
and Hercules is naked also –
that you would expect
with such a virile giant –
he slays the centaur, Nessus,
half-man, half-horse;
look, Hercules draws back his famed club,
ready to smash his victim's skull.

Time has not bruised the calmness
of the centaur's face;
his eyes and mouth,
teased from the stone so skilfully,
show quiet acceptance of a fate,
soon brutally delivered;
he stands in this moment forever,
balanced against eternity.

Next – a sudden realisation!
there are letters within these images as well;
they stretch away in bannered lines,
words perhaps we can understand:
the professor rounds his mouth on them,
savouring their fullness, their Latin cadence,
ready to make utterance
in his learned way;
to him, the words are like sweetmeats
fallen from the weighted table
once laid here with scarlet bowls and finger cups
and silvered flagons lapped with wine:

time has chased away
all but these stark, angled strokes beneath,
yet they may give meaning now
to the frail, frozen figures they rest upon
which we have so lately viewed;
their sound, when spoken out,
will disperse the long-barred darkness
between that first jewelled light,
which saw this writing made,
and our own day's dim incertitude.

This word *Caepio* is likely the owner's name –
or so we are told by our scholar who has traced the word out
with his fingertips – the sun's rays
are crowning the prof's head with gold
as if in glory at his ideas – the first injection of humanity
he has made amidst this ruined wasteland
of tile and stone and drifting dirt,
ageless and soulless, without evocation
of the crowding people who once dwelt here
with all their loves and hates and fears,
at a time when we, watching now, so enraptured,
had no more consciousness than a rock,
undreamt, unthought, unknowing.

Caepio is linked here with *Fortunata*,
our teacher continues,
at least that is how these letters may be read –
he waves across them as if swatting flies –
perhaps she was wife and mistress of this house,
indeed, the names, so closely bound,
show the two were possibly newly-wed,
and this mosaic, the wealthy in-laws' gift:
it would have cost a bob or two!

We titter obligingly:
our mentor has had his say,
and climbs from the trench to our applause,
jangling his car keys in his hand,
his sun hat tilted from his sweating brow:
the crowd relaxes, stepping back,
we hum like bees, earnest in our conversation,
satisfied by what has been revealed to us,
being here at the sharp end of discovery.

A media lady, lushly moulded
in tee shirt and calf-length shorts
is hosing the mosaic with her camera,
sucking up its pictures that may be
spewed out tonight in tv news:
we shall watch with excitement
at having played a part, if only as spectators
of this present and this past,
hoping to see our faces on those screens
that are always with us now
in whatever space we fill:

we have made a living frieze
around a pavement long since dead,
the life it saw, its gaieties and grief
stilled in the heartbeat that comes no more;
the patient hands that shaped this art,
now but a hollowed scoop of dust.

I return on a day of drifting rain:
the grass is grey, the trees
where we parked our cars that afternoon,
stand like men in line, darkly alert
to see why I trespass in this field:

there is no welcoming now,
of crowds and posters and fluttering signs,
hands waving to show me where to go:
the mosaic, recorded, drawn and photographed,
has been returned to the heavy earth;
only a square of weed-hung ground
shows where once it spread
in all its splendour, newly found.

Yesterday is no more and cannot come again,
whatever our imaginings
and our fond recall:
time is but the hammer of our pain;
it has no mercy.

Yet I see the house take form before me,
its roof tiles glowing in the evening light:
the sun hot all day, the dogs pant by the door,
the flowers in the courtyard bend their heads
for thirst...
and here comes *Caepio* with his face so red
to water them with his slaves in tow.
And *Fortunata* has had the house girl sweep her hall,
and oil her pavement against the summer's heat:
she changes to a scarlet robe,
and lies upon her bed,
with aching head...
there are guests coming tonight
to view the mosaic, drink, and make much talk,
how Rome has declined,
its manners worse, its politics unsure.

Just like our own world, I think,
and walk away.

ROMAN VILLA

The pale face with beetle eyes
hovers above the line of walls,
and pits, and banks,
and neatly sectioned earth,
and, blinking against the veil of years,
says with sucked-in lips,
'Them Romans knew a thing or two',
then pads away on gym-shoe feet.

Oh, good! Oh, fine!
I'm so pleased you said that,
and did not dwell with detailed book,
peering at drawings and numbered plans,
'working it all out' with intellectual zeal
and 'cultural awareness,'
rather at some gathering you proclaim,
'Yes, the Romans. I know them well.
Such fun. I love their bath-houses and their orgies.
Saw 'Claudius' on TV, 'Gladiator' too:
why they came here to rainy Britain,
we'll never know.'

Am I then lost in a conceit?
I am drifting on the fevered air
where wind-caught trees
shake their green hands at me
I am falling away, with half-closed eyes,
deep in the mystery of all living things –
Who breathed here? Who saw? Who felt?
What triumphs were there? Who gained? Who lost?

And as my pulsing mind
touched back onto the lost soul of age,
for a tiny instant,
I knew and understood,
like a distant star, seen clearly, then gone.

I swear I glimpsed time in that moment,
overcome,
reversed.

ROMAN ROAD

There are other feet on this road than mine:
I cannot see them;
they tread within another time,
which I can never reach, however hard I try,
although we are travellers side by side.

The way points before me,
straight and long,
to a rampart of hills set against the clouds,
where the sawing wind
sends the black rooks swirling high
above field and wood.

Who are those beside me now?
I feel them close.

A jagged hollow within the grass
showers out nuggets of chalk and splintered flint;
here, sweet Lavinia might have turned her ankle
or bold Marcus, falling, grazed his leg:
perhaps they sit on the roadside bank
gazing out, as I do, at the distant sea,
seeing the beaked galleys racing in to port,
their oars in unison, whipping the waters white,
like the legs of frantic caterpillars
pecked by birds:

or the shepherd comes with steady step
to fill the roadway with his flock,
and cause the rider on his blowing mount
to turn aside, shouting angrily. He holds
messages in his saddle pack for the Legate
in Londinium, and must not be stopped
on pain of punishment, such as those viewed
by cheering crowds on the arena sand below:
he passes by at last, with threats most hideous
called out behind his rearing horse:

the shepherd whistles his dog and takes from his sack
a round of cheese, from which he breaks a piece
and feeds the grinning animal, just by the milestone
that once stood here, but has long since been taken down
and smashed to pieces for a cottage floor,
it being exactly seven thousand Roman paces
from the forum of Noviomagus,
where too I live.

HAT HILL

In the woods
a fussing wind has piled last season's leaves
in ditches old before these trees were born;
their seed was brought by men
whose ashes lie below:
winter will freeze upon the mould
and bind it hard; yet spring sleeps within,
its green jollities concealed.

Sullen is the earth, dark and decayed,
the cattle at the field's edge browse in mud
seeking the hay the farmer has brought:
steam rises from their breath;
the trusting eyes watch me unblinking,
yet I can bring them no comfort,
only tell them of their distant forebears
when this land was of Rome,
but they have no interest.

In the bole of a fallen tree
I pick out a piece of hard black clay,
from a pot a slave may once have held to his lips,
testing the flavour of the dish
he has prepared for his master:
there was a house close by, you understand:
when the field was ploughed some years ago
its floors were found; the cows stamp over them now,
between the *triclinium* and the *culina*,
unashamed of their intrusion.

I tread more softly, thinking of the spirits
that might share this air with me,
wondering at their secrets,
wishing them to show themselves and speak:

perhaps they do.

THE BURIAL

(Wiggonholt Common)

When we buried him here
the high air was laced with mist
that dripped on the mourners
like a weeping veil; the first of the women
placing the mace between his white fingers,
its red-chequered staff bright against
the grey body cloth and the black harness,
with the dulled bronze of the axes
and the flint-headed arrows set in the clay;
and we handed down his drinking cup
and placed it by his face,
then dug out the earth in a circle about him
and made a great mound above
to tell the ages where he rests.

From the ridge top, the land falls away
over all his dominions to the distant hills
beyond which foams the sea at the edge of the world,
out of which armed men may come again,
now our king is dead:
he fought them, and we by his side,
in furious battle by the winter marshes,
where the waters twist out like serpents
between the silvered river banks,
reddened with the blood of the many fallen:
we missed a harvest on account of it
and were hungry for a season:

the bones lie there yet, we would not burn them;
we left them for the wolves and the crows.

And now I come to be the ruler here.
I see they have placed a seat close by
where I may sit and chase ancient dreams,
long vanished in years,
expecting the past to rise again and consume me,
as it surely will.

STANE STREET

A tree has fallen,
the road is blocked:
send to the *curia* for a gang of slaves;
they will clear it fast and mend the way,
so time can march by this place again:
life will then resume its endless flow
into futures that no dreams know –

the future that is my today,
thinking back on the Roman rule
that built the road, and laid it bare
upon the same earth I see,
under the same wide sky.

I pick my way around the shattered trunk;
the clawing branches rear at me like snarling beasts,
unseen hands grasp vice-like at my feet,
my face is slashed by vicious whips.

I decide to battle no further against forces
so set in their determination against me.
I retreat.

I wonder if they will ever open up the road again,
as it has no use now, just as a haunt for deer and man,
and far more the former than the last –
I watch the deer here running free,
as they once did before the Romans came,

then Rome passed, and others arrived,
to follow too along this road,
and vanish into time;

yet the deer remain.

WHITEWAYS PLANTATION

This wood in sunlight seems a delicate place
once I have crossed its boundary through the whiplash
    screen
of brambles that I might think are set to guard it,
for here, most clearly, was a sacred space;
how could it be otherwise? –
    I am amazed no dabbler in antiquities has declared such
    of old
    or modern archaeologist defined it from his technology
    of plugs and wires that probe beneath the soil.

A hollow way points up the hill towards the summit crown,
passing between two mighty ditches gouged from chalk;
each would have taken many hundred hours to dig:
I can see the muscled flesh now hacking at the ground,
the heavy troughs of flints hauled upwards and emptied on
    the banks,
fires blazing, white smoke rising, a camp set out nearby
with deerskins for shelters raised on poles,
pennants streaming out in the gusting wind;
the women are working preparing food,
with children beside them tumbling on the grass
until called to sudden order: be still! Tolfwyn, Heiren, Myru:
the King is coming!
Into the glade he rides, the sun on his helmet in an orb of
    gold;
Myru hides her eyes, it is too bright for her, the face too
with its curling moustaches and blue patterned cheeks;
all about him fall to their knees, yet the workers labour still:

the King is pleased; a drink is poured for him in a wooden
    tankard
as large as a tree bole; he quaffs it in one measure and the
    people cheer.

I tread as gently as I can: I feel I should be bare-footed
on this hill top beneath the trees, for we worshipped our gods
    here,
long before the invading Romans burnt our groves;
at night our priests could count the million stars
and make charts of what was to be, and saw our own death
    too,
yet our blood still flows on. And now in these great ditches
only twisted branches of yew and oak, brambles as thick as
    the wire
a whole generation died upon, and no one here but me:
the universe spirals about me and I am alone.

THE COIN

At the yew tree's gate
the old world begins –
it has never died –
its furrows line the soil
like lids of eyes;
here, the people lived and grew their corn,
penned their cattle against another's raid;
you can find their banks upon the hill,
and the curving ditches of their homes,
where the fires were lit and the ale tubs drained.

One ruler was greater than the rest,
and laboured his men with whip and lash
to mark his land;
mighty his works, carved from the chalk;
at the river's bank, on the high ridge scarp,
they proclaimed his name,
yet none knows it now.

Brambles, twisted like wire,
and palisades of jagged wood,
beset me:
I step upon a slide of flints
where a tree has fallen;
in the soil, round and perfect,
I spy the chieftain's head.

In the museum,
you can see him now,
denuded of his power,
and lonely, I would think,
a mere relic,
fit only for study.

I wish I had left him there
beyond the gate
in the yew tree's shade.

HERCULANEUM

What colours, what fragrance,
what waters jewelled with light,
were lost here when the sun was ended,
all these lives stilled at a heartbeat,
all this brightness failed in the mountain's mouth,
flowers, faces, eyes smothered by night.

THE STAG

A stag bursts from the brush
that lines the winter fallow,
its antlers raised against the greying sky,
scenting the air, standing grandly alone
at the field's centre, awaiting the chase
that will not come, now the hunters
with their hard faces are dead
and lie here amongst the stones:
once with their flint axes and yew-strung bows
they would have pierced it and felled it,
cut it open and taken out its eyes
to give to their priests, who had a temple here
on the crown of the hill amongst the woods.
I walk there now.

The dying leaves shiver in their last extremity:
it is the long years that hold me, and their silence:
they capture me more securely than the stag,
which has passed from this place.

EARTH, ROCK, LIGHT

The earth is not grand and full of pomp;
it needs no ceremony: when we die
we pass away with little fuss,
no grand parade of mites and dust
to see us off, only that Man himself
will lay down flowers and raise a stone or two
in our memory, which the earth can bear
without complaint: it already holds a billion, trillion
forms of life within its rocks, the very hills
are made of them, all that solidity beneath our feet
was once a moving thing, of little toes and tails
that crawled within the swamp-green sea:
today, we plant such creatures deep into our throats
at expensive banquets laid out beside some exotic beach,
where sun-tanned mortality sweeps in on painted boards
and torches flare against star-lit skies,
while a white moon stares down,
seeking out those souls that God bestowed,
but finding only blackness there –

as at the beginning, as at the end,
and so continuing
through time immeasurable
until the first fires, the first light,
when all shall start again.

WE WEEP FOR THE DINOSAURS

We weep for the dinosaurs,
the scaly, muscled flanks of the great ones,
the spiky claws and beaks of the smaller,
those with skeletal parchment wings that flap and fly
over the columnar trunks and broad tufted fronds
of the dense, drumming forests
which we now dig for coal, if we are allowed:

we weep for all the life that was,
extinguished in a moment,
feeling an affinity with its fear,
that our living too might soon be laid
down into a geological age,
and given a layer and a name
that sandy-haired aliens of the future
will long pore over,
once the bombs have struck and we are blasted away
into a shining core of nothingness,
which is all that shall be left of us
apart from a rusty staining of the rock,
as the asteroid extinguished the dinosaurs.

Only, who will they be in aeons to come
those beings who will puzzle over us, dry-eyed?
Not even God's angels will weep for His creation Man,
which would destroy itself.

OLD PHOTOGRAPH

When we go backwards
we see the future more clearly,
when we look forward
the past becomes blurred,
like an old photograph creased and torn –
the boys in their peaked caps,
the blue gabardine raincoats,
the neatly-tucked scarves,
the long, uniformed line passing down the hill,
passers-by nodding and smiling,
'the boys from the school, they keep them well there,
how I wish I were that young again',
ladies with wicker baskets born in 1896,
and we not understanding the long grind of age
that we would face too.

Where were we going?
no photograph can tell me:
our future seemed indisputable then.

BENEATH THE TREES

(West Chiltington Camp, 1941 – 2021)

Beneath the trees
the light trembles
like swirling green water,
the heat heavy;
the piston beat of the sun
is drumming at the earth driving all to shade;
even the birds are wearied of song.

I push aside the brambles and bracken fronds,
seeking what, I do not know,
but surely there will be some sign left
of those men, now eighty years fallen
into history's deep, remorseless pit:
yes, here a stub of red-brick wall
rises out of its bed of clinging nettles.

In these woods they laid out their camp,
set the nissens in neat rows
with tracks of concrete to their doors;
dug in the armoury and the generator,
laid water mains to the ablutions block
and sewage pipes to the latrines;
built the guard house by the gate,
where the mirror-booted soldier
raised his red and white pole
as the grinding lorries, and trucks and jeeps,
despatch riders, corporals, sergeants, and generals,

came and went about their business of war,
consuming them all to the very last detail,
the typewriters clattering out the orders of the day,
the requisition forms, the training programmes, the
    movement reports,
the requests for leave, the names of those who had sinned;

for there was nothing else then,
only the present that might last forever;
but the sun sank and rose and the future returned
to this day when I come here too,
beneath the trees:

so now I must pass as well,
and who will ever recall me or say my name;
no flesh that knew me,
no trail that marks my way.

I leave these few words instead.

FUNERAL

Down that last corridor
littered with light,
they bore him,
into the street
where the people clapped
and called 'God bless you, sir';
his medals on his oaken chest
shining out like stars, not his
to take off and polish now,
the frozen white fingers at his side
locked for eternity, and no more parades
or bugles calling against the dawn.

All his days are gone, shut in earth,
days of monstrous fire and thunder
along the white ribbons of the shore,
the exploding clouds sown with steel;
he sees them no longer,
he has found his rest:
of a million others,
he was the last of all;

and we are much the less for his going;
he told me once he had lived long enough
and did not 'sit easy' with the modern world,
for today we have only nincompoops as rulers.

The Last Post they sounded that day
was for England herself.

THE VETERAN

He sits bent forward in his chair,
his blazer a little worn,
the red beret on his head
dusty with the years,
yet the winged badge is silver-bright
catching the sun:
what does he think seated there?
all that chatter about him:
he fumbles with his hands,
pulling at his tie:
have they offered him a drink?
he should be drinking too:
I would be honoured to buy him
whatever he wished.

Laughter around him, glasses raised to lips,
the skirts of ladies swirling by,
they wish him well,
one thanks him for what he did,
takes his arm;
he looks a little anxious, bemused,
yet is used to this now
and mutters something in her ear;
she laughs: what did he say?
I wish I had heard:
children, curious,
look up at him with round, wide eyes,
dogs too, they pant at his feet.

They are playing wartime music,
a singer croons of bluebirds and white cliffs:
what is he thinking, sitting there,
his head tilted to one side?

Strange, he knew a Cliff once,
was in his platoon,
drank with him in many a pub
in Salisbury during training;
in '43 or early '44, it were;
jumped into Holland with him,
only he were killed the next day,
did not come safe through, as he had,
with only a bullet in the hand:
his fingers play upon the puckered scar,
he has been lucky, that's for sure,
about the very last.

My, they make such a fuss of me,
like a bird in a cage:
can't complain, though.
I'd go again, if I could.

THE LADY CHAPEL, ELY CATHEDRAL

In this white, cloistered cell
where time twists tediously
like a dried-out cadaver spun on rope,
we who seek the place
shall learn of that unhappy age past
when they hacked away the bishop's nose
and sawed the halo right off
the Virgin Mary,
by the doorway
above which the Green Man grins.

Still they come, by ones and twos,
creeping by with eyes lowered,
as if embarrassed
by what passes here, or did so once,
for few have understanding
of this most fragile dust.

It is all a jaunt for them,
something for a dull afternoon,
particularly to light a candle, which is fun,
to hold it out and pretend belief,
glimpsing in the flame the power of prayer:

and I see it true –
as if through clear glass,
a light shining out
so very pure,
it strews diamonds on the stone
about my feet.

PEOPLE WATCHING

The heads nod by,
each one its own universe of conjecture,
each one a cosmos of shifting stars,
whirlpools of glinting lights and colour
in bright uplands of revelation,
or of blackness that betrays
the deep abysses of doubt;

and so I watch them pass,
they turn and twist,
the faces pucker and peer,
some laugh through white gates,
that glitter skull-like –

those I fear.

MORE BLOODY SUN

More sun,
more hot, bloody sun,
the only weather, it seems, the forecasters like,
standing there before their graphics
in bulging dresses and florid shirts;
you see, they all think we wish nothing but
to sport on beaches in merry throng,
rubbing grease on each other's backs,
like basking seals, but without their beauty.

I long for the rain that blows like powder up some country lane,
sending the leaf tips quivering,
swirls over hill sides in a moving breath,
trembles on the larkspur and the foxglove spikes,
relieves the heated brow,
and perfumes flesh with scented drops
like an elixir to renew our wearied world.

Only an illusion, for the storm clouds
soon hover black over Trundle's top:
of a sudden,
the sky is filled with silvered spears
to wash the parched earth into mud
and flow away like thunder.

I run with the rain,
following the milky white streams
that gurgle joyfully by path and chalky ridge,
through blowsy fields and brooding woods,
soaked,
but happy as an idiot.

I live! I live!

THE RAIN

The rain has come:
its waters lie upon the earth;
they dissemble its colours,
make liquid its solidity,
confuse my plunging feet.

The clouds dissolve now,
like a tattered army
seeking a new sun:
the white blood of the past
is all about me, washed anew:
I hear the scream of field flints
by the hedge,
piled high for collection.

All across the drowning land,
the valleys are shouting out their fear
at time's long remorselessness;
they see the graven shadows of what has been
and is yet to come.

I shape my lips into an O too
and pass over the earth,
the mud clinging at my heels,
knowing soon I must stop
and embrace it.

THE STORM

All day the wind has howled and shrieked,
like a giant child in tantrum,
flinging out its muscled arms
and seizing hold of spires and roofs,
trees, garden sheds and playground swings,
sending them all a-tumbling down
in gleeful swirls of poisoned breath,
withdrawing for a while to sulk
then returning fiercer than before
to have a second turn at smashing toys:

yet, am I alone in kinship with this gale? –
feeling it scourging at the ground,
sweeping the dry earth clear,
booming between the buried tombs,
returning the dead to life anew;
long before our present age
of phoniness and pretence

has passed one second, now all has gone,
the glittering screen and obsessive phone,
cut off like ancient dust:
where is the water, wood, and fire,
the light of new day, will they come again?

The great switch is thrown back
and we are returned to chaos,
we mighty ones who promoted
such conceit, we are lost,
far worse than animals,
until this storm has passed.

WITHIN THE SHADOWED DOWNS

Bury me lonely,
bury me bleakly,
bury me cleanly

within the shadowed Downs,
and there time shall lie with me,
its light extinguished,
a candle to trouble me no further,
of all things that might have been
and may yet be,
within this circling universe of stars
inestimable to man;
some say God holds us in His hand.

I have seen the light of all these days,
too long for further questing,
and shall be happy now to trust in God,
and close my eyes.

WONDERING

All this wondering,
all this crazed contortion of fact and memory,
this attention to devious detail,
these dark rivulets of worry that sour the soul
can be ended in a moment;
no worry then, for they will exist no further,
those cares of the world,
who should rule whom and who should plunder,
show sin or virtue, love or hate,
shake down the trees or cast aside the sun,
such things will no longer be of concern to me,
and if they were, I would know them to be
irrelevant, inconsequential,
I would wonder why they ever bothered me at all.

Even the domed universe
filled as a swirling sea with multitudes
of stars and nebulae and foaming galaxies,
endless and unchallengeable,
a cosmos so vast, time has no say in its proceedings,
it too shall be without meaning,
for it will be no more or ever have been,
as a drop of rain is dissolved away
into nothingness;

And what of God?
of God the Creator, I do not know:
God is all around us, they say;
God is a certainty of light.

REFLECTION – TRUNDLE HILL

I feel a hollowness upon the hill,
as if its blunt fist, thrust against the sky,
has stilled the air – a vacuum
that the past may fill.

Dark clouds are gathering,
a warrior host borne over the sea
in ships that sail with blackened wings
like carrion crow:
they will root out our dead,
they will hang them up anew.

Where are our spears?
Where is our armour, bright as sun,
the belief, the will, for our defending?
I see nothing,
only the slow slope of this hill,
falling into the unknown.

I turn my eyes upwards
and they fill with the rain:
this ending is a shaming
beyond understanding.

It is not I who stand here now:
it is the long dead,
and their heads are bowed.

LONG DOWN

When I came out upon the Down
I met a man with two sticks,
one on each side, planted firm
in the ground, as if he wished to grow
his remaining days from them,
leaning there, bowed to the wind.
He said to me, 'do you walk far?'
I replied, 't'would be further if I had your two poles,
one in each hand, instead of my single stick
that was my grandmother's; yet the wood
is sound still, stronger than my legs,
and she lived a good age and saw out
two great wars, three if you include that
of the Boers, but who remembers them now
or Mafeking Night or Baden Powell?'

We parted, he seeming to understand
the intention of my words,
or perhaps I fooled myself
and he thought me over-strange;
yet he wished me well on my journey
and I on his, and we set our courses,
he to the east and me to the west;
soon he was just a flicker on the ridge
and I beneath him deep in the earth
where once the ancients dug their flint,
the land about me without end,
and I just a pyramid of dust.

BOYHOOD 1950s

In the long cheeriness of the hour
we scraped and scrapped,
boys in grey shirts and shorts,
socks at half-mast, knees muddied and scratched,
the blood, a badge of pride,
with snake-head belts of yellow and black
and a school cap worn low over the ear
(when snatched off it flew well over a hedge).

We were beaten at school, scrumped apples and plums,
and, when it snowed, stamped out slides on the pavement
to make the grumpy old man at the corner house fall,
but he never did, and walked our dogs
leaving their droppings everywhere,
and never cleared up the mess, as they do today,
but then we knew little of sex either
and nothing at all of transphobia or diverse society,
or video games, or social media
or saving the planet, and we respected
our teachers and policemen although we called them names;
they sometimes clipped our ears,
and woe betide you if you burst into tears;
it was not done to make a fuss or wail.

It was always sunny when sun was needed,
and when it rained, it came in torrents
and then went away, never hung about to weep at you
like a girly might, and our games

were all of soldiers and beating the Germans;
we built dams across streams and blew them up with
    fireworks,
until the farmer came with his shotgun and frightened us away,
and we dug tunnels on the common to escape from the Goons,
and did infantry crawls and threw stones for grenades,
as our fathers had shown us, for the War
was still only a heartbeat away;
and the Army lorries, filled with conscripts,
came into the town, and we ran behind
shouting 'Up the Navy', or the other way around,
as the occasion suited, and they would throw pennies at us
and tell us to 'sod off'; and there were kitbags on the trains
and men still going off to war, in Malaya or Kenya
or some other foreign place of which we knew little,
only of Mount Everest, which had been conquered by Hillary
    and Tensing;
we had followed their climb every day on a photo of the
    mountain
stuck up by Miss Morgan on the schoolroom wall.

And the Coronation came and we sang 'God save the Queen',
with the Union Jack at every window; ours was on a pole
    outside,
flying the highest of them all,
and we were so proud of our country:
it brings me to tears to think of it now.

LITTLEWORTH COMMON

I remember the pond on the Common;
it had two ducks upon it and was hidden by tall bracken,
so you had to beat a path to it over a low ridge,
and running nearby, a mossy ditch, sharply-angled,
the correct depth for a curious child,
left over from the war, I would think;
perhaps the Home Guard lay there and watched the road,
the air spread with vapour trails high overhead.

We lads from Hillbrow Road played our war games here,
stalking each other, with bracken stems for spears,
crawling through the green light of the undergrowth
like the jungle soldiers seen in films, or as our fathers told us,
although often reluctant to speak of what they had seen:
soldiering is not a game, they said, but boys must learn for
    themselves,
as every generation has done, and ever will, it seems.

And the sky was always blue with streaks of white cloud,
and the smell of the crushed bracken a drug filling the
    senses;
time hung still in the sunlight:
childhood was forever.

I came here with my father once –
at the pond's edge stood a lone silver birch;
I can see him beside it; the bark of the tree

flaring like a torch, catching the sun, and he smiling;
all was happy then and all in order:
it is hard to return the world to such perfection.

I returned to the Common the other day
after near seventy years distant in other lands,
and could not find the pond again:
the place was overgrown with thick bushy trees
as far as the Portsmouth Road and the roundabout:
it was impossible to search further:

but no boys played there anymore,
that was clear.

THE PASSING

In this graveyard
the spent mortality of the town
awaits its redeemer,
ever patient, together with the worm and snail
and the bright birds that chatter amongst the fir trees
by the fence,
yet the yew that overlooks the church stands silent;
its feet were planted before these walls were built:
once they worshipped here with fires and roasted meats,
sought eternity through the fermented flesh of toadstools;
that was long before the Christians came into this land,
and what more was done we cannot say:
it would be indecent even to speculate.

I enter the church now,
struggle with the door latch – is it locked? –
no, it opens of a sudden with a crash,
waking the long silence, sending the ghosts to hide;
the greyness of the sky seeps in behind me;
I smell the dampness of stone and wood,
see the piles of prayer books by the font
the tattered notices on the board,
a history too of the church, its edges curled:
ahead, the altar cross is watching me like a light,
brighter than any window despite its coloured glass.

The memorials tell me of some who worshipped here;
of Lieutenant Palmer who gave his life on the Somme,
his mother hands down her loss to us in stone;

she lies outside, her grave is choked with weeds;
the world fell away from her that day the telegram came:
I trace her stone most gently with my fingertips.

And Robert Hudson is remembered here too –
'he loved England and worked hard all his life,
often against great adversity':
I wonder what he did and how his patriotism was shown:
he would not recognise our world today;
the England he knew is now buried as deeply as its dead.

I weep for all their passing.

REMEMBRANCE

I saw you in this silence, for you are always there,
where once we drew across the grey veils of the night,
and talked of times that have gone;
and do so now, as shadows on a sunlit path
between the flowers,
touching the weeping blossoms as we pass –
you and I.

And the storm is in my head,
and high, and I am crying out for you
who are lost;
and I am so alone in this night,
with nothing but the blackness and the rain,
and the feel of your hand remembered,
and your eyes.

Still me, and hold me,
and give me breath to live,
for you are from me
a short journey, no more,
of going and return.

EARTHAM HILL

They were shooting on Eartham hill
when I came over the Down;
in black lines against the fallow,
a dog attentive at each pair of feet,
its jaws grinning wide and pink:
I passed them, raising an arm,
but none signalled his notice of me;
in stern silence they stood, like sentries on duty,
awaiting the enemy's rush against the sky.

I was almost at the ridge top
when the shooting began,
in volley at first, then firing at random,
the birds bursting into feathers and falling,
dogs darting to gather them,
their tails flourishing like sails;

and all around me life was pushing up
through the dead winter's soil,
and the sun bore down upon my shoulders,
heavy with light:
I stood there on that hill
and I watched them dying,
those beautiful creatures of air.

THE BEACH

Today is dark and drizzling,
the distant sea, like rumpled grey flannel,
unbroken by the white of wave or foam;
at the beach, small breakers
nudge listlessly against the groynes
where the seagulls sit, pondering on fish,
eyeing me as I clash across the shingle;
I am not a creature of scales and fins,
and nor do I bear any manna from the shore;
they soon lose interest:

and I see a dog by the water's edge;
it is old and trails its owner,
head down, not heeding his commands
to 'come now': the sea is oblivion,
it is a motion swelling to infinity,
the dog would rather shuffle its feet here
a while, before treading into that eternity;
the shingle of life lies in banks steep to climb,
yet it paws at them, stone by stone,
nosing at shells and ribbons of green weed,
until helped up, kindly now,
by one who clearly loves it, its two-pronged master,
who must himself be fearing the tides to come;

as I do too, watching, wondering at the pain
that is involved with living,
when dying is so easy; yet like this dog,
thankful for each day that is left to me;

and so I journey on.

PEACE

I wish it could stay like this forever,
in this moment, with the shadowed sunlight on the walls,
floating in a depth of peace
far out of time's dull motion,
a sense of eternity, perhaps.

Is this where the mind shall wander when the body fails?
If so, it is not so fearsome as the prophets tell,
those doomsters of punishment, of fire and hell:
such rest is not to be derided; God will not admonish us
with wagging finger, nor will He come in bucketfuls of laughter,
wearing a funny hat, a T-shirt marked 'Saviour'.

God is peace eternal;
nothing less.

RECOLLECTIONS FROM BOYHOOD

All day it has rained;
the tree tops are clouds
where black rooks sit
in gloomy meditation,
their prey swims in water below:

the grey puddles link arms
in a sea beside the houses;
a lorry sends its wave against the fence,
where Mrs. Elwes has just passed;
her brolly is ripped upwards by a bluster
of the gale, her skirts flap immodestly
about her knees: a schoolboy notes such things
and writes them in his book for future
contemplation;
and now the gutter overflows beside the window,
it races like Niagara down the panes,
and father curses the work that must be done
when the sun returns.

Such memories I hold
when looking out on that street
which was my world when young;
here all things were made,
all dreams fulfilled:
it was the Oval for our cricket,
a battlefield on fireworks night,
an arena for our cycling tricks.
I wonder at the patience of the adults

whose gardens we trampled,
who tolerated our calls and whistles,
and let us take the apples from their trees,
thinking we were not noticed.

Today, our crimes would be worse, I'm sure,
for our innocence seems golden now:
what deeds will those with knives and drugs
wish to recall, come wind and rain,
and age?

FEAR

We are at the end of the years:
the gates break,
the days are freed into chaos:

the earth is brittle with the ash of the burnings,
the ditches choked with rubble;
sculpted hands that held scrolls lie at our feet;
ivy cracks the stone,
words are ground to dust:

and still the singers wail their tunes,
contorted and frenzied;
our eyes are blinded;
by the bright gallows of the sun
they writhe upon:

their song is of love,
but all I hear is fear.

WALBERTON HOUSE

The grass waves a yard high,
with ferny bramble, sharp and rank,
choking the soil, deep-matted with weed,
beyond the ha-ha from the house
that stands white-walled, lit by sun,
with pillared colonnade at front,
from where a titled lady once looked out
at her lawns, neat-striped and set with croquet hoops;
here, song birds pecked and bathed
in the stone basins she placed for them:
her bones rest now at the church beyond the hedge,
to which she walked each Sunday by a hidden gate,
veiled in black, her prayer book in her hand.

Soldiers came, Canadians in '41, Americans next,
in huts across the ha-ha, in the raggedy field;
the concrete floors can still be seen, once carefully scrubbed,
now overgrown, half-buried in earth: the barrack-master
would have died of shock at the desolation he would find:
you can see the names on the gate post carved in brick,
'P.Hall from Manitoba, 'Pete Krupa from Tennessee':
the officers' space was in the house,
their bedrooms up the flighted stair that merits
a mention in Pevesner's work,
the ballroom, now flat no. 9,
formed the mess, the planning room was where
the lady dined in formal state, her maids
in starched white aprons, wearing caps,

her footman in long-tailed coat, who carved the meat
ever since her husband died: he had been a banker in the City,
worth £7000 a year with railway stock, until its sudden fall
that caused his heart attack.

And now I live here too, the breathing grass about me,
the yellow sunlight framed by watching ghosts:
in the frail flicker of light left to me,
what death am I to meet? – today, tomorrow,
whenever time decrees:
will I be borne to that same church
beyond the secret gate?

CLOUDS

No less the light in Arcady
no less the glittering sky
where the clouds sail out like galleons
upon seas of billowing white
and the depths of blue are vaultless
beyond man's poor art to contrive
out of all thought to journey
into such spaces undefined
where the start may prove the ending
and stars dissolve to dust
this rapture of clouds in glory
above a shining sea.

THE ESCAPE

(Tenby, 2022)

The world is mad;
there is no escape from it
other than the grave,
which I would forbear a while,
the Lord being willing.

What then to do?
The crazed seagulls sing and prance about me:
in their shrieking I hear the full inferno
of that cruel insanity which rules our day:
there must be quieter places than this sea,
with its misted island across the strand,
hulled by monsters, where the deep fish breed
and make their claim to land,
this solid earth to rest their bellies on,
these hills that bear the torment of the wind
and bring its wailing into silent homes.
All life came from the sea, they say:
Is that true? I do not know.

I met a man today
close by the railings that o'erhang the beach;
he was bent upon the bars,
wedged tight against them
like a great folded pin,
of the type that once held nappies in place
when we were babes;

(such things then were not in plastic vacuum packs,
but I digress).

He said to me, unasked, this man,
winding his head round on his wiry pinnacle of neck,
'The monks sing psalms on their island still,
you have to pay them money now at the gate
to hear them, but it is worth it, every note is
sweet as honey and the singing never stops,
not even when the Abbot calls all to prayer,
or so it is said, but I never stayed that long'.

'You see those rocks' – his shining finger tips scored
a shape against the sky and I made out
the white, bursting waters that he meant –
'seaweed hung over them when I was a lad, as slippery
as an ice slide: we used to scramble there, you see,
when I and my mates went to become monks too –
but they wouldn't let us in'.

'We were not old enough', they said,
'but not too young for the Army that next year
when the soldiers came beating up for volunteers:
I wouldn't have gone had I not been so bored here,
full of sleep at midday and life trickling out of me
like a punctured bag,
and no deeds done worth the calling;
so I went off to fight instead,
and now look at me. You wouldn't think, would you,
I once marched into Jerusalem bearing the country's flag?
Strange the world, isn't it?'

'But if I had gone for a monk, now likely I would be dead,
mortified by prayer earlier than my soul,
which yet sings on in this great song of life.
Don't you give up singing yet, my friend'.

I saw him walk away, until he was but a crooked shadow
scarce darker than the grey town wall:
he stopped to speak to another passing,
but that man waved him on,
impatient perhaps to keep to the daily madness
from which for a few jewelled moments
I had quite escaped.

ON THE HOTTEST DAY

On the hottest day in history
I fell asleep,
and when I awoke the sky was yellow
and all the grass too,
and the trees were stretching out
thirsting leaves, fervent for water:

there was a long silence
upon the earth, and nothing moved;
the stillness was complete,
other than for my own cautious tread on the path to the
    church,
where the walls slumbered shut and the windows shone red –
the second coming perhaps, in flame and glory,
yet the dead lay on untroubled;
there was no stirring beneath the ground,
although the very land itself seemed tilted to the west
before the sun's deep anger
that only time would quench:

at the far horizon,
where the seas beat solid on an iridescent shore,
all the birds were gathered into one long song,
crying for release:
but only man was free,
and he moved not at all:
it was so hot.

England died this day
I remember her once
in restful showers and foaming fields,
her woods as verdant as life itself,
but singed a little now,
and crazy with the sun.

THE LAST RABBIT

When I went in search of the place
where the last rabbit screamed and died,*
he had been dead for a very long time;
they had taken his body and fixed it
with formaldehyde
and placed it in a gallery with other old things,
under a sign, 'The Very Last Rabbit of England',
and next to him was the very last
butterfly and dragonfly and sparrow and curlew,
stag beetle, squirrel, red deer, and water vole,
every bird and insect and four-footed thing
of 'olde England', which was what that gallery
was labelled in quaint old-fashioned script
like an ancient monument seen on a map,
and most of those have gone now too
under the spreading concrete and brick,
which is called 'Meadow View' and 'Sweet Pasture',
the last being the exact place where they killed the rabbit
and sent it into hell,

and where we follow
blinded,
without thought.

* *'We are Going to See the Rabbit'* – Alan Brownjohn

THE WORLD HAS CEASED ITS TUNE

The world has ceased its tune,
the music is seldom sweet now,
the notes jar black and white,
the melody lost, and all are poorer
for the change, however we see ourselves
or in what form we have our being:
the land is dark under the remaining trees,
but darker still where the earth has soured,
and we must go from where the mad ones live
to find ourselves a new sanctuary of light;
yet, where can that be?

The plains are filled, and the mountain sides,
the valleys choked where the people dwell –
all their little gardens are but weeds –
the air heavy with turbine blades, bright panels flash
along the rivers, where the one sure output of the multitude
drains away towards the seas, in stinking coils,
pestilent on the land like serpents' breath;

and there are no horizons for us now,
only those we are given by our distant lords,
who are everywhere about us on the many screens
that make up our days, and from which we gain
our information on the way our planet points,
or which part is doing what to whom,
and why we might join in, for that would be right –
    would it not? –
irrespective of what we actually feel;

for we know we are of little count really,
despite what they assure us and ask us for our views:
their voices sound out at all our corners,
above us and around us, from beneath our feet,
and even our thoughts are theirs to command now,
they must be the absolutely correct ones
or they will be held before us to be revised;
if not, it is the pit of cancellation that awaits us,
and that might mean our ability to live at all:
they have not started executions yet,
but I am sure those will come next!

Gone are all our brave people, our benefactors and thinkers,
their statues are overturned, their genius reduced
to mere conformity, with *damnatio memoriae*
for the most incorrigible and evil:
some of my favourite names were on that list,
but I dare not say so now.
I am just one unit of expense and trouble,
instantly removable, instantly forgotten,
that and the whole world it once was mine to love:
all is inverted, Satan rides triumphant at the crest.

This England Now

pass the wine, stoke up the fire
make ready the servitude

who are these who come
to watch our new registry
in a time where history has ended
where nightmares have replaced
the sure sweetness of living
where the flanks of devils run wet
with sinning

where foulness finds shrines in new religions
made hasty with grieving
turns the waters red with bleeding
wipes out the innocence of children
sweeps all into perdition
this broom of the sky
these chasing clouds licked with thunder
racing to oblivion

who will cease it
what prince of hope in bright armour
will come from out these shadows
into sunlight fresh and laughter bright
glistening like meadow grass swept by rain
jewelled in merriment

there is none

better then that putin's bombs
should find us too

VIRUS TOWN, March 2020

Only the wind struts and leaps
in the spring town,
quiescent in sunlight:
the long street lies empty
and the castle on the hill frowns down
puzzled at why the ants below
no longer swarm about its feet.
I look at the buildings as if I have
never seen them before –

the charity shop, once Yate's the Grocer –
you can still make out the name above the door –
the queues were long here in the war,
when the enemy flew against us visibly;
his bombs threatened our quailing flesh,
but did not dissolve our inner cells
with a plague unseen,
a cowardly way to fight, that is,
rightly banned by the high tribunals of the world
when spread by Man,
yet Nature's own aggression
is exempt, it seems:

and here is the school, lying silent –
no jumble of cars now with kids unloading,
eyes on phones even before Mum has said 'Goodbye'–
so I can see its doors clearly, the date '1902' above,
a bright new century opening out,
under the reign of the King Emperors,

soon to be split asunder
by wars far greater than this present pestilence:
'Girls' and 'Boys' , I note too, carved in the stone:
how long before those identifications
are chiselled out for our own age of
dysphoria?

A policeman – I swear I have not seen one for years
except for a blue blur of passing light –
has just asked me why I walk here when I should be indoors
shut in and isolated from the infections that stalk
these streets? I tell him laughingly
to mind his own business, and am reprimanded
with wagging finger and informed I must listen
more carefully to what is said to me
or I could be fined or even imprisoned.

And so I go home,
my obedience freshened.

I shall applaud as well whenever I am asked.

TO THE NEXT BIG WAR

All the children are crying in this hour;
the bells are sounding out like a gong
that is beating for war; come quickly or
you will miss the first serving;
on the menu today is roast and grilled flesh of many races
in all manner of preparations, chopped or diced or shredded,
and delivered to you in any way you wish,
if you are still able to digest them.

The young men are coming to this feast,
as they have always gathered when such calls are made,
and there is something noble in the sight,
the long-shuffling lines eager to sign away the lives
their mothers bore them; once it was flat caps and bowlers
    they sported,
now the baseball cap makes the major crown, its curled peak
scrawled with 'Cool Dude' or 'Nike' or 'Amazon';
it seems we are warring for the corporations, and not our
    land,
which may be theirs already, anyhow,
yet still we go;

for there is something instinctive in what we do now,
it is in the very collagen of our bones,
that makes us come out from the shoddy twilight of our
    dwelling
and seek a greater cause under which to live and die,
a purpose to justify our inheritance;

and, if there is a generation to follow,
we will give them some proper history at last,
enough to fill the media channels for a year or two,
should there be any left to view it.

HORATIUS 2022

The old wars are returned:
weary with history, I see the actors
play their parts, as they have always done –
the demons and the heroes,
a man who sacrifices his life
for a nameless bridge;
its successor now will be known after him,
stuck up on bold signs by the motorway carriage:
what glory!
better he had ploughed his fields and raised his children,
yet not to be:
he met history head on
and punched it in the face,
one of the immortals, he:
in another age his name was Horatius.

WHAT THEY HAVE DONE

They have taken a perfectly good country
and knocked it into pieces
for one man's vent of hate –
a man called Putin,
not a name to give your dog:
it is strange how many evil men
have two short syllables
for their identity:
Hitler was one, and Stalin, of course,
then Satan himself; Beelzebub, beside him,
sounds rather quaint, but not our Putin boy
smashing up factories with his tanks,
houses, hospitals and churches too,
like a naughty child scattering his bricks
because his mummy won't allow him out to play
with the bigger lads stoning the ducks
in the park.

The analogy ends here –
while the young Putin's rage
might have been ended by a well-judged slap,
his older self holds his thumb ready,
hovering above a big red button marked most clearly
'Fire!',
which would blow us all to
perdition, should he press down on it –
men, women, children, dogs and cats
and all our history too, in one great storm
of insanity:

for this is what the world has become, hasn't it?
quite mad:
we debate whether women
are men, or vice versa, turn our armies into adventure parks,
filled with girls without ammunition,
question the essence of our past
and say we are guilty of many crimes,
while the real world grows in evil about us
and we are quite unprepared for the devil that will ride down
    on us.

While the politicians are safe in their deep bunkers,
delivering their homilies, wearing the right coloured rosettes,
    flying rainbow flags,
we have not even a siren to tell us of our danger,
no organisation of relief, no nice round helmets marked
    ARP,
no 4-minute warnings, that would now be reduced to two.

We are expendable. The elite will scatter themselves across
    the fields like turnips,
growing again, flourishing with their old enemies,
while we are long-dead, mere ash beneath their feet,
and this time they will not even recall us –
no monuments for us and long lists of names:

of us, there shall be no memory at all.

WAR

The silvered flights of rain
strike upon my face
but do not pierce me,
neither my eyes for seeing
nor my lips to tell,

yet in Ukraine, shells
are falling in shoals
to burst open skin and bones;
the spun hair of children
like gossamer
on a devil's breath,
driven to oblivion,

laughter and lips,
eyes and ears, now as
senseless as the force
that threw them there,
out of mind and reason.

The utter uselessness of existence
strikes into me at this time.
What to do? Is the answer more war?
More death?
When the clapping of the politicians
turns to silence,
and the sky rains ash,
then will it stop?

Who knows?

ON EARTHAM LONG DOWN

A Reflection on Ukraine

These white lines of chalk are bones,
disarticulated, dissolved within the muscles of the body
into earth, where the great flints lie;
to be seized upon by other hands
and pounded into weapons –
points, coshes, knives, and axes,
each able to open up a pulsing brain
with commendable dexterity
and spread about its juices –

and so begin the first wars,
whose dead stand before me now:
they have never ended,
for it seems a condition of man to fight,
women, too, the bearers of life,
they lie equally in the hallowed ground
of death amid the flowers,

where the bird song is so tender,
the air cries with the rain,
weeping for the dead of the old wars
and the old dying,
and the killing of the day.

I HAVE SEEN A COUNTRY

I have seen a country,
full and fair in the morning,
with courts and castles,
rich markets and bustling towns,
content enough in a place its own,
sour rapidly like sun-drenched milk
left long to stand;

and in that souring
has come foul baseness,
and all the pretty folly of pretence,
which declares truth a rusting sword
and virtue a monument overturned:

now Diversity rules in unchallenged splendour
and the great god Inclusion raises his multi-heads,
while our goddess of Green makes her ecstatic progress,
paraded by children before whom all adults must bow;
Pride too marches out to make further strange conquest,
its rainbow banners fly above every hall:

where once there was certainty, peace, and comfort,
there is now dissension, the whip and the lash:
those with power who have created the anarchy,
ever flex their muscles, pleased enough with their work:
we who are left, cringe, bullied and silent,
frightened to speak: we recall the old days that were,
and retreat to our caves, beseeching the last god of all
to swing his scythe soon,
and let us escape.

A SUMMER MORNING IN ENGLAND STILL

A beautiful sun rise:
how many more shall I see
in such bright definition?
looking out at the beech trees filling the morning sky
with their dark-green crowns of summer leaf,
and seeing the fretted shadows of the palings
that line the gravelled path,
passing from the old houses by the church
to the busy village street,
where the queue for the Sunday papers is yet five deep
to read the news of another broken government,
then fall asleep.

BINSTED

If you would come,
be quick!
for the planners have laid down their mark
and soon will bisect the village that trembles here
with a deadly road,
so all those silent, box-like cars
can run in straight lines, pollution free,
blessed by bishops for their electricity,
and arrive five minutes earlier, at the most,
from other blockages to west and east
that yet will obstruct their streaming way:

you must believe, all this is needed
to save our Planet from further decay,
if not our minds that pulsate in pain
at the savaging of what we hold most dear –

the bright fields on which the concrete will be poured,
the dark woods whose secrets children now will never know,
the Norman church, whose groaning walls
will bear the ponderous weight of desolation,
the graveyard where ghosts may rise to watch
how these new woke despoil the earth,
yet rather retire to their long sleep,
than see these vandals at their work:

in their great-great grandfathers' time
such berserkers were slain in bloody battle,
for the land to them was a most sacred thing,
to be blessed for its bounty, not torn asunder
under the power of that rich god Progress,
whose vanities oft run amok
to the satisfaction of his worshippers –
those who are fed by him;

or so the villagers think,
and who cannot agree?

IN FURREY TIME *

In furrey time
when the wind blasts at the beeches,
I let my cocoa leak onto my chin
and, closing my eyes,
dream on of princes –
superbus est miserabilis –

Do the wild men range in the green wood still?
Is another front opened against the sun?
questions to answer when the storm has stilled;
then the quiet eye to find its vision,
immoralis bona est
ad maiores opes
for the greater good.

Laughter is shrill in the wilderness,
laughter like rain drops pattering our heads,
streaking our hair, making waterfalls of noses,
puckering lips in distaste,
laughter that makes mockery of jollity,
curling up our voices, wishing us silent;

like straw men – the stuffed men of Eliot –
with hooks for their feet,
so they may be hung up in the rafters like bats,
old-fashioned and leathery, with the cares of the ages
about them, wrapped as any other object

---

* *furrey*: from Old English, 'wild', 'crazed', 'uncontrolled' – pronounced to
rhyme with 'Surrey'.

to be thrown out on the road,
with the durex packs and the lager tins,
and the plastic containers of rotting chicken
bought in the store by the park,
which the seagulls eat to stick in their throats,
so they can no longer scream at midnight –
quelle vie! as our Gallic friends might shout
across the water, when they are not smoothing the way here
for the very many who drool for an English home:

mein Gott! are they all mad?!

* * *

I stir in the morning,
sniff at the grass, as dry as Sinai,
shaved to a yellowed bowling green,
studded with the thrust of daisies
that yet press themselves out,
believing in the power of light:

I bundle my pyjamas into a ball
and throw them at the painting of Madonna on the wall;
if only the world were a pop song,
then all would flow in creamy frippery –
a world without any dark blockings,
or of rulers, kings and peasants,
bright songs beaming everywhere in idiot sunshine,
life a game that children play – 'ring-a-ring of roses' –
ha, ha, it heralded the plague, so you got that wrong,
didn't you? you smooth-tongued, talking girls
with your straight, white hair, your lips reddened like wounds,
only you will never bleed. And who comes next?
It is the sand boy straight from hell,

who would bury us in his nonsense deeper than a tomb,
with teeth whiter than ice blocks,
flashing a smile of ease that maddens me,
the confidence of a grinning imp,
released from the earth to do mischief
incomparable.

* * *

Wait for the news. Slide open the picture can by the wall
and see what comes out.
Death in a city.
Louts in a train.
Police on their knees, praying.
Leaders at a party in the mountains,
to which they have sped in glistening comfort,
with engines that chop away rain forests
more speedily than Mrs. Huggett can ever do
with her coughing tumble dryer in the shed,
struggling to clothe her daughter, so she can go to school
to learn how to copulate without danger.
What does the prince say about that?
He is a spirit wafting on water,
more certain of his genius even than Jesus,
who recognised His sins and died for them,
and for all of us too. I don't think this prince
would die for anyone but himself, and then he would seek
to make a film of it, so as to carry his comforts
into the afterlife.
But who can blame him for that?
Is heaven graded, with clowns at the top
and the rest of us tottering below,
balanced on pyramids?
I fancy so.
I must speak with God, so He can put it right.

FURREY TIME FOREVER

Furrey time has come again:
in furrey time the past slides backwards:
it was the fourth dawning then.

Long-necked reptiles slope against the sun;
their time is short: the comet is coming
to blast all life into nothingness:
God will be busy with his clay
to start again, as He moulds the monkey
Man.

The fifth dawning is ours: we are the monkeys
of furrey time, clambering up our poles,
swinging out on branches,
dropping down on other heads
to kill their owners, if we can,
squealing in our fun.

This is the history we make,
of monkey-man: once of the angels,
but that chap Darwin polished us away
into his filing cabinet, and when he drew us from
the drawer again, we had a different label,
one that made us grunt and howl and jabber,
using the eruptions of our backsides
in preference to our mouths,
the former having gained a new role in our feelings:

our first design now –
when we stop long enough from eternal war –
is sex and the condition of our genitals,
in as many ways as can mutate
from out the frothing swamp pool
that we have turned the world into,
when we aren't destroying it
with our machines, anyhow,
servicing those myriad swarms
of us that balloon everywhere –
fat balloons, they are, in the main,
in all colours of ugliness,
having tidied away God's other creatures
into the zoological park of extinction,
although they held secrets of wisdom and beauty
we could never emulate,
not from the first dawning to the last.

How many monkey-men and their mates,
queer, gay, trans and all,
can you get into one footie pitch of land?
500? 5,000? 50,000? 5 million?
time then to start hollowing out the earth
to fit them all in,
and chuck in as well as many play-stations,
smart phones, porn platforms, game shows, rappa bands
as are needed:
they should fill a crater or two,
in the earth's crust,
all crammed in somewhere near hell's doorway.

And so we await the sixth dawning,
backwards, the seventh is the end,
for that is before God Himself was born
out of chaos: and chaos shall breed chaos
unto endless night:

the light that was given us
is abandoned:
God is tired of it:
and all those bishops, imams, gurus, wellfulness prophets,
and the rest,
said little that mattered:
it could be asserted they made it worse

Furrey time is long dead soon,
or now:
whatever sits within your head.

IN MEMORY OF A JACK RUSSELL

What fun we had, little dog,
you who rolled with me, spun with me,
walked down the long hours on hidden paths,
saw sunrises and sunsets,
barked at the wind,
slept under the stars,
kept loyally at my feet when you were on duty,
yet had your own way, your own spirit
when the bounds were loosed,
and sprang out at enemies and chased them into ditches,
cats at the most, yet squirrels in plenty,
and things much bigger than these for whom you showed no
    fear,
tractors and motor cars and huge growling lorries,
you would have rounded them all up
and sent them into purgatory, your dreams were huge;
and you rest now in a space so tiny that I dug for you.

I placed a rose upon your neck
and spread the clay over you,
and I wept.

THE SKYLARK

Up, up I gazed against the sky
and ever sang the lark,
a grain of frantic melody
against the blue vault high,
dissolving within the tuneful air,
too soon to catch its cause,
yet sung in praise, I have no doubt,
of the creator it would find:

it would take us poor earth-bound clods
a whole cathedral-full of prayer
to match the insistence of this creed,
such certainty of God.

VISIONS

So hard it is to pierce the light
and seek past forms from out of night:
what is it you wish to find –
a baby's smile, a young girl's laugh,
a perfumed lady sweetly dressed,
flowers that colour meadow grass?

A street of stone is what I see,
the gutters foaming white,
nailed boots that kick and scrape
in shattered rhythms at the gates,
a dog too with three legs lost,
broken-backed against a cart,
its mouth an oozing pit of blood,
its red teeth wedged apart.

TO EDWARD THOMAS

On Shoulder of Mutton Hill

You, who walked these hills,
your mind furious with words,
careless of fold and furrow,
your thoughts finding pleasing harmony
with the breaking twigs and powdered leaves
of last night's gale beneath your urgent feet;

until all of a sudden you stood at the hill's edge
and, raising your hand to shield your eyes
from the imperious glare of the rising sun,
you surveyed the land below you
in all its manifest wonder of field and copse,
and half-veiled lanes, white as dust,
like the bloodless veins of ghosts,
deep borne and peaceful
in the early breathing of the day.

Was it then you bent to scoop up that handful of earth,
saying out loud to all living things about you,
whether man or woman or child,
bird of the air or fowl, fox, or badger,
beetle, bee, or the tiniest ant,
that this England was worth fighting for?

And so you went away and did not return:
it goes beyond reason by those who do not understand
why such a sacrifice should be made by one
who did not need to fight;
but I think I know,
standing in your place balanced on the hanger's side
and seeing the same beauty as you
and feeling the same great solace,
to be swept away too most surely
by all the gales to come.

FALLEN POET

When I came down Mutton Hill
it was at a roll; several times
I turned, less dignified
than a porker pierced upon a spit,
its meat rotating for some merry feast:
my slide was ended by the poet's stone
hard on the shoulder of the hill.

How Thomas would have laughed
to see the presumption of my fall
beside his chiselled words,
'I was tired, so rose up again';
and that I did, and took my course,
humbled now from all pretence,
my thoughts a-tumble in that Hampshire wood.

THE LAMB

A lamb comes bleating up the fold,
white as innocence,
fearful of the yellow sunlight
that floods its eyes;
and I think: what for?
this swirl of dust
was once dead rock
and shall be so again:
will life then resurrect itself,
or God abandon his sullied world
and start again somewhere else? –
where no frightened animal,
need cry out for its mother,
in terror of a journey to be made
far from the good shepherd
in green pastures.

I share your fear, little lamb,
could you but know.

HELPLESSNESS

This bird is sick or old,
about to die;
it stands helpless by the path
and does not move when I pass;

but I see its eye
fix on me and then away:
it has no hope of salvation from me;
there is no Pigeon Health I can send it to,
no potions to give it, no feathered nest
for shelter:

perhaps, at least, I could save it from the cat,
who, with ginger limbs and lithesome prowl,
is king here when the sun grows low,
but even that would be troublesome:
surely I am not part of this nature,
destined to unfold.

Their eyes watch me, the weak and the strong,
and I must turn myself from both.

THE FLY

The fly irritates:
it swoops before my eyes
and occupies the telly light,
part of 'The Chase' in this moment
of its notoriety, answering questions
on how many bugs make up a summer,
until I reduce that number by one at least
with a swinging blow from a paper roll
of daily news; in which I have just read
no life has yet been found on Mars,
although some goggle-eyed professor,
remains most hopeful.

The existence I have just taken from our Earth,
on another planet would have been
the universe's sensation,
but here, just one more piece of bally nuisance,
now deceased:
I drop its tiny body in the bin.

REPORT TO THE DOCTOR

(Perhaps on Zoom)

When old age comes,
it is an army that invades me,
first my feet, then advancing to my knees,
makes its main encampment there,
with many entrenchments that cut my poor joints sore,
allowing them little power to kick
the infiltrating enemy out.

Soon the army will fire off its cannon at my heart –
the gods willing, they may yet miss –
but skirmishers have entered my head instead,
where they take root, hissing in my ears like seas,
registering my decay and likely signalling my decease.

RHYME

A person asked me,
Why no rhyme?
I replied,
It is no crime:
A garden of a thousand roses
Can be sniffed by girls with purple noses,
Yet, a flower smells fragrant too
Using a nose of other hue.

ON RECEIVING THE RESULTS OF A POETRY COMPETITION

The competition results have come
and I have not won, or
been commended, or
even mentioned in passing;
so I shall write no more
is my decision;
what I see, I shall keep to myself;
why would I wish to share it, anyhow?

A poet who sulks is no pretty thing!

I'M DONE WITH WORDS

I'm done with words,
all those packed, princely pipers of purpose,
the shrilling similes, the verbose verbs,
the stuttering descriptions,
of adjectival phrasings, set out as starkly,
as devils' claws raised
against a sun-rich sky,
where swallows swoop in endless circles
above the swelling vortex of the night.

There are simpler things to write of – surely?
babies' smiles, for instance,
or blushing apples seen against the deep-green grass,
the drone of honey bees,
sea waves, white with foam
far away upon the dreaming bay,
where sails are lit in orange and pink,
and languid mermaids comb out salt-wet hair:

such things, it seems,
come from a time more innocent than ours today,
almost to be pitied that men once held such dreams,
for now it is fierce frenzy that moves the jettied world,
confusion, objection, and prejudice,
are but some of its qualities I could name,
if I dared to and had the gift;
but my box of words is quite emptied now:
I do not have the vocabulary
to set this world down.

WHEN THE QUEEN DIED

When the Queen died
it rained all the day;
the gutters gushed with water
washing the lanes white,
filling them with stones:
the birds hid in the trees,
and there was no song;
the very earth was stilled,
only the rain ran on;

and I walked in a drudge of leaves
mulched by the hedges,
where brambles still bore
the fruit of summer passed:
what now?

The new King is born;
the wheel turns on,
as ever was, out of time and trust;
yet, there is a weight upon me
I do not understand;

and I would walk high in the hills
to find a reason,
but know I shall find none,
only that in the east the sun is rising
and the land shines out again,
like the dream it was.

9th September 2022